Dark~Sky Society

New Issues Poetry & Prose

Editor	William Olsen
Guest Editor	Nancy Eimers
Managing Editor	Kimberly Kolbe
Layout Editor	McKenzie Lynn Tozan
Assistant Editor	Traci Brimhall

New Issues Poetry & Prose
The College of Arts and Sciences
Western Michigan University
Kalamazoo, MI 49008

First Edition, 2014.

ISBN-13   978-1-936970-27-8. (paperbound)

Library of Congress Cataloging-in-Publication Data:
Hopper, Ailish.
Dark-Sky Society/Ailish Hopper
Library of Congress Control Number   2013949847

Art Direction	The Design Center
Design	The Design Center
Production Manager	Paul Sizer
	The Design Center, Frostic School of Art
	College of Fine Arts
	Western Michigan University
Printing	McNaughton & Gunn, Inc.
Cover Image	Sarah Skeen, *Untitled.*
Back Cover Image	Alexander Torrenegra, *Obama Inauguration: 1.6 Miles Away from the Capital.*

Dark-Sky Society

Ailish Hopper

New Issues Press

WESTERN MICHIGAN UNIVERSITY

For
What we do with
What gets handed down

Contents

Acknowledgments

Many thanks to the following publications, in which some of these poems first appeared, sometimes in different form:

Agni: "15 ½"

American Letters & Commentary: "On Being Crazy," "Silver Gelatin"

American Poetry Review: "Romanticism," "Home of *The Quiet Storm*," "Cyano-"

The Baffler: "Song of Whiteout and Blackache"

Blackbird: "Circle in the Grass"

Copper Nickel: "Self-Portrait as Smoke"

Elective Affinities: "Gestures of Progress," "The Real Abolitionism," "Honk Not (A Patdown)," "Dream, Technidifficult"

Harvard Review Online: "The Good Caucasian"

Ploughshares: "Like Light"

Praxilla: "Lincoln's Hands," "Closed Space #634," "Closed Space #1,348"

Tidal Basin Review: "Emancipation Test #672," "Sketch for a Narrative, Well-Meaning," "Emancipation Test #54," "Plight of the Overseer"

Tuesday; An Art Project: "The Crooked Hour"

5 AM: "Trad"

"Variation, After Heavy Rain and Thunder," "Letter: Guilt Trip," "Mnemonic," "*this beautiful needful—*," "Post-," and "After History" appeared in my chapbook, *Bird in the Head* (Center for Book Arts,

2005). "Dark-sky Society" was published by *Split this Rock.org* as Poem of the Week.

Gratitude also to the corporation of Yaddo, Vermont Studio Center, the MacDowell Colony, Goucher College, and the Baltimore Commission for the Arts and Humanities for the time and support to complete these poems.

My thanks to CW and JH, without whose careful teachings this book would not be possible. Thanks to JAY, for true brotherhood. To TSE, for your eyebrows. To ACB, SM, AH, JF, JR, HB-N, SC, and MM, for Beyond the Call. To my friends at Goucher, Because you Know. To the Posse, the Sisters, the Mommas, for watching my back. Thanks to New Issues, especially DSJ and NE, for taking a chance. And to my mom, my dad, my bro; to Dan, and Tomas and Ethna; for the One True Thing.

...whatever else the true American is, he is also somehow black.
—Ralph Ellison

I.

Self-Portrait as Smoke

From a broken storefront window, smoke
        canopies two young men

      who kick another's caved-in body

[helicopter   circles]

then raise and drop a block, concrete
    on his head
        While men, then women, step past, *to*
rectify, by emptying
        store shelves

I see this on *camera*, Latin for *box*
    or *room*; in this case, some white

people's living room. *Terrible*,
    I say, & change

        the subject, as if my body were
           diffused

[leaves   wind]

        dispersed, ribboning

while a man is dragged
    from bed

[curtains   parted]

windpipe crushed
        collar stained, hands jerk
                and stray
        While men, then women, tear from his pants

                [damp   night]

their souvenirs, *to*
        preserve
            The flash-

bulb pops; the splash
                kerosene

                [door   behind]

        and then the flint
the arcing match—

flame

Home of *The Quiet Storm*

—WHUR FM: "Sounds Like Washington"

Yesterday, in the alley, a man
was found

hair stringy, matted
hardening in the sun
like mud

Where dandelion
and burdock rise, fill empty yards

& bind the wheels
of soundless cars

Spilling from a pile
of plastic bags, his body's

a waste

my neighbor says
of a perfectly good

white boy

But today, in the shade, young men
buff and gloss

all around, cicada song

in waves, the way
a breeze might come

High-pitched wail
that almost drowns

the radio: *Just bees*

and things and flowers

Closed Space #634

—Baltimore, 2009

In a diner, my friend and I
        sit beside a white man, whose mouth
is frozen open

as if to speak
        [refrigerator hum]

while next to him, a black man
looks away

They float
beside our table, in a wall-sized photo

      feet hovering
                [static]

         above ketchup bottle
      twin stacks of jam

From the bar's TV, a man

in tall grass, night sky
explains   *Everyone*
hopes
        for that second chance

And this was it

View of the Capitol from St. Elizabeth's

Space is nearer.
—Robert Lowell

i. Lincoln's Hands

Dream city   I climb

          an eyelid's
molten curve
drop into a mouth, cavernous

burnished aluminum
teeth, pressed

to the small of my back. However cold
the *skin*

it is a thrill

to touch
Man, *Awakening*

while we scale his face
and hands

Capitol city   We'll
          vaporize

if the bomb comes

say the grainy films
radiant

with *aftermaths*
Implicit

handed down

like the length and shape
of fingers

color of my eyes

City of windows   Rhetorical
          cemented-in

the view
from St. Elizabeth's, where my dad fills
notebooks

Blue ballpoint
slanted shapes

whose meanings
have all

peeled away

Dw dr
Dw dr
   he says, eyebrows raised

Another thread
I hold, not knowing

what it leads to

City of memorials Mute
     white façades

granite, pantomiming
loss

After the bomb, they'll all
vanish. Gone

Lincoln's
marble hands

that drape

colossal armrests. Missing
chiseled wave of hair

laid across

his forehead
We

cannot hallow

this ground
the new
                absence

might, like Lincoln
say

Or, perhaps

            Begin

again

ii. Letter: Guilt-Trip

"on Saturday JANUARY 11UP FOR BREAKFAST   9
1;30   0   1/14   CENTRAL

FIDELITY

CHECKING TWO E WEEKS JANUARY 25

ON YOUR CALENDER AND MINE
FEBRARY   AFTER JANUARY,
the folll   FOLLING WEEK   FEB 4   5

AILISH   VISIT
FRO M   "

iii. Disappearing, Inc.

In the film, the man
who's chased

does not
scream, keeps

his features
hard—*Boy,*

wipe that—
taught, even by

his mom, *Come here*
look down

       When the bus
doors open,
my father climbs

then someone pushes, yells:
Hey

somethin' wrong?! as the bus driver
explains,

to my dad, again, what coins

go where

              There is

Its lessons written
everywhere.

The man
on film

does not escape; in frames we see
his face
filled only with

imagined life.

And my father's: a page
that flutters

blank. Once, there was
they say

beautiful ink laid there

Variation, after Heavy Rain and Thunder

Here's another message

from pain

From a power line, a robin sings
after the rain

chl dee   chdl
chl dee   chdl

goes the streak of sound, insistent
as a rusty hinge

It's the same

Then   longing

as if in a window's condensation

Traces
makes its shapes

and letters

II.

The Good Caucasian

[It's] the ghost in me coming out.
—Lee 'Scratch' Perry

When forty acres have besieged
my brow, and a mule

and a winter, cold
as Ice Cube, I try

a remembrance of things, floating past—
Miss Daisy, and her necklace

of fingerpointing   Title pages
On the South   now squares of ash

centers embering
If memory be a mountaintop

mine is hidden

by fat, puffy clouds, and other
symptoms. But, when dis-raced

in men's eyes, and by time—
dust, the centuries—I will admit

impediment. My body
is where we are held

My eyes
have drawn

your shape
and you mine. Not

I Have a dream

A cold, cold feeling

Aubade with Lines from "Let's Get Small"

In the club's flashing lights, a man brings
his hips to mine, hands float

                    to my waist
              Uh uh
Tell em what you feel like doin, ya'll

No pale, etiolated leaf, in a room
of wine-dark foliage, I am like

Now what you gonna do?
the true freaks, outside
              Let's get small!
—Cicadas

their high-pitched whine, vibrating
through tree limbs—Stepped
                    Once you get started—

from glass-like, ambered
              garments

all-nymph

                    Bodies, luminous
              you can't stop
albino. For this brief hour

the unrecognizeable, alien tinge

of a body
            before

color

Dark-sky Society

Every time, Kenny says

I look　　　*at you*
I see

Princess Diana

His skin, ginger
mine, peony

And, between us, now
the color line

no static beam

More like light-
　　　　　　bomb

Blanching
our star-dark

Our
lumen-*natural*

Ways to be White in a Poem

Tension makes
a form resound

and so the many lines I am told
not to cross

Do not go out alone at night
Do not call attention to yourself

Closer to the color line
the more I am
            White girl

fool

It is a while before
the other girls

correct me, gently. Good timbre needs
more air
            Shout out!

Muscles flex, quick-shift
            I stomp, impious

impervious, now

Do not dance suggestively
Hold a stranger's eyes

That first day in the gym
I asked the row
                    Could I

        thinking
about cheers

elbows sharp, foregrounded

        feet, cloud-
                        stepping

Never of
                    A cheer

        as the body
        went up

As if I were. Were not

        Branch creaking

Rope taut

And, maybe you, too—
whoever you are—reading this

flicker

Do not touch
Or eat

Their food
Do not drink

From the same cup

Pax Americ-

—After Martin Luther King, Jr.

In many of his speeches: *Magnificent.* He is naming, but also calling,
something buried, a giant. In the room, *Forth.* But Giants aren't real,
are they. Migrate or hibernate, the fictional creature might have said,
pondering. My therapist, Joseph Conrad, feels I have *become, in a*
manner, the slave of a ghost. "He's a good man," say my friends.
In my heart, an image in oils: A sailor, looking overboard, to see,
in the darkness, the shape of Force. It's Lawrence Olivier, as Crassus,
There is only one way to deal with Rome—he says, to Tony Curtis,
as his slave—*You must not only serve . . . Also, you must love.*

Gestures of Progress

Every figure, a field

even the pietá
Death's gesture

Eyes always
closed
though every cell in her
    Touch

        touch

Every portrait, a breaking

Pink wedge, a thigh
    torso, a goblet

Always the mind
        They

How far will you go

I re-gessoed
    And, still

    it showed
        through

What a line surrenders

With each
stroke

an eye blooms

The End of History

i. "this beautiful needful—"

Brain damage
is like water seepage

through computer circuits
where the water goes

information
disappears

But it can leave islands
untouched

A synapse fires
through unspoiled matter
he says

Finch
Finch

in words collapsed
upon themselves. Says

Father
Father

And I imagine him
then

preacher's tall son

wandering red clay paths
listening

and looking up

for small, quick shifts on branches

ii. Letter: The End of History

"THE PRESIDENTS and   dates of DEATH

7. Abanaman Lincoln   (1861 – 1865)0
8. A Andrew Johnson   (1865 – 1869)0   in
9.
10. . Ulysses S Grant   (18869 – 1871)   in 1885
15. John Fiquarte Kennedy   1963
        shot   in 221963

        Martin Luther King Jr,
            shot   on April   in 1968

        RObert Francis Kennedy
        WAS   1968"

iii. Mnemonic

Sable for its face, *cobalt* for chest and wings

and ballpoint words, spiraling

around it, as if its nest
was going up in smoke

His full name, his wife's
his social security number

street address, telephone number
of the house
where they once lived

The rest
the vast

swan-white
pocked, and thirsty page

untouched
Draw a picture

they said

of all that you remember now

iv. Letter: The Right to Code-Switch

                    "VVVVVVVBBBBBBB
                    FOR BREAD ORGANGE
                    JUICE TWO CANS SOME MAYBE
                    TV DINNERS

John. Please do what I do!

I went to the store. I went to the store.
It is cold today. It is cold today.
MeRRy ChristMas. MeRRy ChristMas

                    BBBBBNNNNNNNNNNNNNNN
                    VVVVBBBBBBB
                          There is strong
                loveTHANKSGIVING CHRISTMAS

                    TO KNOW   , remember
                      , john has quick,
                          but

                                  NO

one can tell"

Divided Interior

—Dublin

After the Rising, looting. The British prop a wounded Rebel,
 just so they can shoot him.
Yeats: *too long a sacrifice/ can make a stone of the heart.* In the
 city named Unvisited.

When Revere called out, *One if by—two if by sea,* he meant,
 Begin.
All signals, a way to touch—*Over all of Spain, the sky is clear*—what
 must appear unvisited.

Because they're hard to see, I listen for the doors' close. In the
 questions--- *So,*
and micro-second's pause, to my mother's answers, *Oh—*, when we
 become unvisited.

Slow-dances in our discotheque: twilit shed, BBC. With a Protestant
 boy, I *let him feel,*
body listening. Then he whispers, *American, not Catholic?* and gets
 unvisited.

Ailish, the codes—*The princess wears red shoes*—seem innocuous as
 children's rhymes. But
symbols seep—*The Catholic one is by the sea*—deep into muscle,
 bone. What cell is not unvisited?

III.

In the Hospital for the Negro Insane

Slave! a slave! Is this a dream—for my brain reels

—Dion Boucicault

i. Emancipation Test #672

Instructions: *Please draw 'slavery'*

(Facilitator: first remove all slavery
from the room)

Score of 4 Drawing of person. Crowds Brown Legs
And Head Around Tiny Torso. In Chains

3 Caucasian Monster. Legs Float in Space, Arms Not Obviously
Connected.
Head is Not Present

2 Drawing Reveals Some Indication of
Tree Being Received. A Rope

Score of 1 Blue or Green Lines Totally
Distorted. Encroached by noise

SCORE

_____Almost the same hardly any better at all a little somewhat slow
    better

ii. On Being Crazy

I can't tell you, you have to see
If tender enough, any touch
will bruise
Now, never think anymore of your place of origin
Beneath "I love," a weight
bleeds through
I'm not supposed to be angry
It's your own choice
Enveloped, body and breath
So that the very veins, like tiniest roots, capillaries
The center of this, unrecognizable
They took her, tied a rope around her neck

*

They took her, tied a rope around her neck
The center of this, unrecognizable
So that the very veins, like tiniest roots, capillaries
Enveloped, body and breath

It's your own choice
I'm not supposed to be angry
bleeds through
Beneath "I love," a weight
Now, never think anymore of your place of origin
will bruise
If tender enough, any touch
I can't tell you, you have to see

iii. Silver Gelatin

[he, as

   a   child

                  held
       by
            —]

[Face]

—a blur of light—

iv. Spell

So many myths

Even death
        Send me a postcard

hard to swallow

Study for souvenir painting
WE MOURN OUR LOSS
Acrylic on canvas

A noose

A keepsake
banner

Is there a formula

Perhaps if

v. Emancipation Test #54

Instructions: *Tell the doctor what you see
in the letters below*

```
A  H  K  W  H  I  T  E  G  L  B

J  S  Q  B  L  A  C  K  V  S  N

Y  Z  C  B  L  A  C  K  M  R  D

R  E  L  W  H  I  T  E  N  O  Q

F  I  D  W  H  I  T  E  L  G  F

N  X  T  B  L  A  C  K  S  L  Y

K  B  N  B  L  A  C  K  E  R  U

S  H  E  W  H  I  T  E  D  F  A

N  W  T  B  L  A  C  K  E  L  H

Q  J  U  B  L  A  C  K  P  U  O
```

vi. How to be Down

Sing
Can't you

Sit

Something

Stand
Happy?

Can't you

Sing
Up

got to
Get get

Happy?

Well I'm so

Down
Got to, got to

Stand

Got to
Down

Get get
looks like

get on

       Up

vii. Sketch for a Narrative, Well-meaning

I draw a cell I draw

The person inside I draw

The cell a person I draw

Inside the person

A cell inside

The cell a person I draw

I draw inside a cell

Inside a person

The person inside I draw

A cell

viii. Plight of the Overseer

> *If you cut your finger, bandage the knife.*
> —Joseph Beuys

Mindset of punishment

Mint mind, set on meant

Punishing, a mind for

Mean, a Meant-ist

A mind

Set

ix. Emancipation Test #78

Please describe your pain on the scale below:

_____The shimmer peeled from a feather

_____ From a hollow-bodied guitar
An abyss

_____ Rusted shut

_____ *Then,*

_____ Metal trees
Roll from place to place
On castor wheels

_____ A cloud
No door

IV.

And beyond, just yonder, a river called Treason to rely on . . .

—Toni Morrison

Cyano-

With other pastel

faces, the old
speakers   weapons

   clothes   *flashy*

hiding
around the table   *I'm just*

saying

Evident, evidence   Theories
Take Jefferson

Even Adams called him *a shadow man*

hushed, bland
like the great rivers, that make

no noise Easy to forget

They're carving

valleys
       Cold, vapor-blue
       outlines

A manners-scape
Those *whose bottoms*

we cannot see

Like Light

—*J.M.W. Turner's* "Slavers Throwing Overboard the Dead
and Dying, Typhoon Coming On" (1840)

How it is that *up*
is known

Here, outstretched
umber hands

punch through   An ocean's
concave mirror

Death's
inverse

universe

But that's
not in

This   view

Just shimmer
Haze

at the edges
Where slip

ships' spires
From flame-

shaped waves
Flame hands

They lean

pull away

Closed Space #1,348

In the famous friendship, Krishna appears
offers Arjuna
[hibiscus, pink blossom]

a life that's truly free

Says, *Kill*

with the sword   *of wisdom*

all your doubt

I think of Keisha, a friend from school
our sweetness
that   *I know*

will not nourish   *will*

disappear
even as I reach for it

In blinding sunburst, Krishna reveals his *true*
self

countless heads
[un-frame]

tender, wrathful

Feet, planted
both near and far

And everywhere
[bright stream]

bliss melodies

Arjuna wanted to see
him, had called
Yet, at this, shakes his head
But, he says   *where is*

my shelter?

now that
I cannot see the ground

"Something that Isn't Real"

In my mother's purse, a wallet, keys
drycleaning receipts

two dog-eared, folded sheets
—Poems, kept

since that afternoon
electric, sun-

lit, when she read

then stopped, hand

on mine. My
long-gone

father, now in
the room with us

when not one thing

Feathers of hair
is brought forth

as if lifting

in the *like* wind

Song of Whiteout and Blackache

1

Well I'm so white,
when the lights go out, I glow in the dark.

So white, when I wear white clothes
all you see
are the stripes on my socks.

White
as the sun's bare rays—iron-heavy
and hot.

White as the grass that's decomposed,
bleached-away
by a leaf pile.

2

Well I'm so black
when I walk at night
I absorb all the light of the stars.

So black—I can't drink milk, sing
White Christmas,
drive a white car.

Black
as a vinyl record—issuing song,
not blood.

Black—as the ocean's
depths, with fish, translucent,
unreal.

Four at 0:0

—*Welcome to the Nation's Capital*

On Sixteenth, the *po*lice
again

hands on their 'nines
elbows cocked

Some knucklehead, says one
tired god

who must always deal
with mortals' errors

ignored the signs
walking the banks

L'Enfant traversed, envisioning
a city, *new*

whol[l]y

At the corner, boys play
buckets, beats

conjuring
soldiers, sleeping

footprints
while on them drips

the rain
in the phosphorous

present
shared seam

I ride, knees against
a motorbike's

cool steel
Through

They forever try
said the traders, *to deſtroy*

themſelves
Through

hilltops, families
who've *made it*, i.e.

away
Through every

thought *This one*
into two, made

That one
Through

The dead bodies seem
in the heat

to move

Through even The
Dream

map's
new center—*0:0*

No battle
Yet not

mustered out

of service
Not free

But, at least
set loose—I split

lanes, like all
the rest

Glide
through dark

Tail lights
burning

in humid air

Dazzle Ships

—RMS Mauretania, 1918

And now the convoy arrives
Hidden
in arcs of light
                    dazzle ships

            they're called
Ten-story iron hulls, dissolved

like mountain peaks be-veiled
            by clouds

Up close, they reappear
                    giant swaths

of yellow, vermilion, tangerine
            slanted planes
                    of royal blue

      Gray metal
            obliterated, made jester

From this hand-riveted, human
lifeworld

is only *Color*

seen

V.

No trace anywhere of life, you say, pah, no difficulty there,
imagination not dead yet, yes, dead, good, imagination dead imagine.

—Samuel Beckett

Circle in the Grass

As a branch is bent, the years
I still have a lot of flashes

Once there was
A tree here, two-story oak

Now, just a circle in the grass
That will not regrow

A battle is indescribable, but once

Seen it haunts a man
Until the day of his death—

Here, there used to be
Footprints   Clothing

Today, the hundredth
Anniversary

       Delicate flakes—
Blossoms—

Here, there used to be

To sleep, I lay down

As a branch is bent, the years

With murderers

Cracker (A Crumble)

I love

a breaker,

But not

A boxer, or beater.

A cracked

Cookie. Crumbled.

A crank, who bleep-

Bleeps

Invisible signals

That

[   ]

Her mouth. I love a

Break-it-

Down. A every-broken-

Part—a

Crumbs, no wrapper,
Cracked-

Up, broken-open—

All-

Out.

The Real Abolitionism (Will Never Make it in the Books)

Landscape *in rain*, the physical body   Landscape *in pain*
the lyrical body   *Broken ink*—a paper page, a missing leg
In both, *the brush skips*   a snowfall's layers of silence
Landscape in breast and rib   cells   of liquid air. Pile of
rounded river rocks   Shaded sapling   confused for

In this place—

Here—

The nightmare body. Landscape in words, gestures. How ink
and water, together, create   *and then*—   Landscape
in silence   *After,*   Mind, like rain, dripping   on beech leaves
Like tented roots   gnarled trunk. Mind, beneath the water's

swirl, untangling   How ink and water, together, create

I need—
        The miracle body. A brush,
            so filled

the paper cannot absorb

15 ½

When
    you're done here,
says the woman,

not recognizing
        her new neighbor, cutting
his own grass.

An echo of, from the kitchen,
    my aunt,

        who yelled, *Jack!*
Why don't you get that
      nigger

to come here,
    and mow the lawn?
        & Later,
an ebony-skinned man came
        in a khaki cap, removed
    at her front door.

A yankee, from DC, I watched
    as if I could discern *the cause.*
All *Progress*, un-
      transformed
      as the goldfinch, when young,

                              dun-
                    colored, early spring.
At 15 ½ I am sure
     I can *get*
              to the bottom

of this, tranquility—blood
                         that connects.
          The finch clings
     —Youth! restless!

                 relentless—
                         to feed
          on towering stalks

that threaten, sway.
          My aunt, old-school,

     Alabaman, jokes and laughs,
offers the man *sweet tea*

     granules, soft now, melted away. A-blur, a blur
                              of *Ours*
          were well-treated, and

                 Blessed
          to die
                 before his son,

82

from river, delivered
to clammy ground.

The finch is willing, will
consume
even the hardest, spiniest
of seeds.

& Only by this
appears, in fall—
Yellow, astonishing

—Neon shock—

Not *new*, just
unthinkable—this one

who is not by past, but

by future, made.

Three Bandages

HUNDRED-YEAR-FLINCH

Dead sister, angry
mother

always with him
So even his smile

twitches

A smile, a wince
a smile

A NEW WORD ORDER

When Ethna, new word-maker, learns her
age   *Teeyoo*

it constellates

                                       Tyoo
Moves
through space
                    : *Well, now, what's* your *name?*

Before: engulfed, afraid
                                       : *Tew*

                        Now, a force
            Two.

a gathering field

ROMANTICISM

In an Oldsmobile's 22-inch rims
liquid silver

                Clouds
                always moving

Clouds

Dream, Technidifficult

—After Martin Luther King, Jr. and P-Funk

I want you to follow me through here
    So wide

They said don't come there
        You can't get around it
But I am here
    So high

They said there is no here
        You can't get over it
But I have been there
    So low

There,

      There,
You can't get under it

      I may not get here
Our only guide,

      But look there
the groove
        Here you are

Post-

He is focused, forehead wrinkled,
lips tentative with the sandwich

of salty, marbled ham,

a fallen frond of hair
over the biopsy's indentation

from thirty years ago,
today.

I savor his careful swallows,
breath's sounds,
slowness. For him

there is no *why?* No *what if*

it hadn't happened? No
suffering.

When he finishes, he looks at me, smiles.
Dw dr

Dw dr, he says. *Daughter.*
I don't know

what he sees, but I return

his gaze.
I return all of it, all

of what he offers, and all
that he cannot,

not questioning, *will it stay*
or, *is it true?* I simply reach across

thought's threshold,
toward

what light reflects

from the sea that joins.

To Ignorance

Entering Penn Station, I see a man, hands
                              tracing the slats
of a wooden bench
          but I keep moving, think, *He's*
                    alright
as departures
                    VERMO—
          HARRIS—

revolve, cascade   *At track*
                Number five
          Stops, in

               Then, I notice: his
          body's still waving

Invisible, the current: thimbleful
          of junk

               steady-swimming
in his bloodstream
                         Today
          someone asks

     why I am writing
about race. I look up

               at the ceiling's false sky
tulled shapes, fatal as hope

I have, I say, a gentle answer

and a tough. Which
    do you want. My head's
        already hurting
   with memory, like

   the time I called
by his first name, my professor
who was black

   or when someone asked
      about my poems, if I would *do*

the dialect

He chooses
tough. And I say, Actually, that one

you have to learn
   for yourself. The station glitters

   with windows,
dark. *How do I*

   look? I say, to my
reflected self
      Keep

moving, says a voice
that disappears
so quickly, it is as if

it was never there at all

The Crooked Hour

After visits to our father
         in St. Elizabeth's

my brother and I
         imitate the patients

Blur our speech, stiffen and kink
our arms
         in mock-convulsion

then dissolve

in laughter   Even
         when watching
Jerry Lewis

speaking for
      kids who have
no future   But

         when a friend's
five-year-old brother
         gets toy handcuffs

for his birthday
         older boys *show how*

         cocoa arms, stretched
behind him

cheek, pressed to wall
                —while everyone, but me,

        laughs
His grin, from start
            to finish, undiminished

Even I, finally, crack
a smile

At what lies, straight

while we
            crooked as light

try to convey it

Honk Not (A Patdown)

Forgive and forbop,

honky. Be-honky bop.

Forgive all fortonk.

Honky? Luck,

until bop-a-tat-tat,

bopgun begot.

Forgive all behonk,

tonky. Behonk or begive.

& Tonk-a-tat not,

little Dixie-tat,

Topple-crats

—O,

even Eye-crat—

Honk not.

Trad

The fiddler starts, with three sharp

notes, and then
the ouillin player moves

the sea, breathes
into bellows
elbows squeeze

as a wave unfolds
in me

my son, beside me, watching, as I watched
mother, grandmother

uncles
Around the eyes, the jaw, same
brimming

cup, same dam
of words

        twigs
in flow   *The past*, a river, moving

—through meadows, made
night-damp—
        into *here*

this room: moist
with heat, insects flood

the light bulb   Where my uncle
says   he's *back there*
          with each sudden noise
cannot stand *small*

talk. Wants a table, peopled
with empty

pints. Wants the old
songs
          to keep away

the sight: an infant girl,   rolled
by a soldier's boot

face-up. Yet, where else
is time

than in song's
hidden cells
A man's

tapping foot—

A woman's voice lifts—

After History

The rain will reach everywhere
sooner or later

Even the leaden
seams

that curl and hide

My tongue, finally at rest

See
                    music

how the iron blooms
in the spring rain

powdery rust
                    of the world

clinging

Notes

Ellison epigraph is from "What America Would be like Without Blacks" (*Time* 4/6/70).

"Home of *The Quiet Storm*" uses lyrics from Roy Ayers' *Everybody Loves the Sunshine* (Polydor, 1976).

I am indebted to Elham Atashi for the phrase, "closed space," used in several titles here.

Lowell epigraph is from "For the Union Dead" (1964).

Italicized lines in "Aubade with Lines from 'Let's Get Small'" by Trouble Funk, on *Say What?* (Island, 1986).

"Dark-sky Society" owes much to David Owen's "The Dark Side: Making War on Light Pollution" (*The New Yorker* 8/20/07); "star-dark" is borrowed from Jean Valentine's *The Cradle of Real Life* (2000).

"Ways to be White in a Poem" was inspired by Thomas Sayers Ellis's "Ways to be Black in a Poem," in *Skin, Inc.* (2010). It is dedicated to him and to Jake Adam York.

Italicized lines in "Pax Americ-" are from Joseph Conrad's *Nostromo: A Tale of the Seaboard* (1904), and a scene famously cut from the movie "Spartacus" (1960), which lives on, courtesy of Youtube.

The title of "*this beautiful needful—*" riffs on a line from Robert Hayden's "Frederick Douglass," in *Collected Poems* (1966).

Some italicized lines in "Divided Interior" ("the princess wears red shoes," "over all of Spain, the sky is clear") are American military codes from World War II.

Morrison epigraph is from "Home," in *The House that Race Built*, ed. Wahneema Lubiano (1990).

Boucicault epigraph is from *The Octaroon* (1859), which was brought to my attention by Daphne Brooks's *Bodies in Dissent: Spectacular Performances of Race and Freedom 1850-1910* (2006).

"In the Hospital for the Negro Insane:" the series title is taken from, but does not directly refer to, the Hospital for the Negro Insane of Maryland, later renamed Crownsville Hospital, which closed in July 2004. "Emancipation Test #672" riffs on the Clock Drawing Test for dementia, in particular the scoring described in Sunderland, et. al. (1983). "On Being Crazy" borrows a title from Du Bois's essay (1923); italicized lines are from Hugh Thomas, *Slave Trade: The Story of the Atlantic Slave Trade: 1440-1870* (1997): "Never think anymore of your place of origin. Do not eat dogs, nor rats, nor horses. Be content." Chekhov epigraph is from "Out Beggary." "Spell" references Kerry James Marshall's "Souvenirs" paintings.

Italicized lines in "Cyano-'" are from Joseph J. Ellis's *Founding Brothers: The Revolutionary Generation* (2000).

"Like Light" riffs on a passage in, and the Beuys epigraph for, "Plight of the Overseer" from Marcus Wood's *Blind Memory: Visual Representations of Slavery in England and America 1780-1865* (2000).

"Close Space #1,348," "Gestures of Progress," and "The Dazzle Ships" owe much to Hardy Blechman's exhaustive book on camouflage, *DPM: Disruptive Pattern Material* (2004).

"Blackache" (in "Song of Whiteout and Blackache") riffs on "whiteache" from Thomas Sayers Ellis's "Marcus Garvey Vitamins" in *The Maverick Room* (2004).

Italicized lines in "Four at 0:0" are from Walt Whitman's *Specimen Days* (1892).

Beckett epigraph is from *Imagination Dead Imagine* (1965).

"The Real Abolitionism (Will Never Make it in the Books)" riffs on a line from Walt Whitman ("the real war will never make it in the books," from *Specimen Days*), and was influenced by a line from Bodhidharma ("Make your mind like rocks and trees"), as well by Fritz van Briessen's *The Way of the Brush: Painting Techniques of China and Japan* (1998): "the lines are broken and the brush stroke acquires an inner life."

Ailish Hopper is the author of *Dark-Sky Society* (New Issues),
selected by David St. John, and the chapbook, *Bird in the Head*
(Center for Book Arts), selected by Jean Valentine. Individual poems
have appeared in journals including *Agni, American Poetry Review,
Harvard Review, Ploughshares, Poetry,* and *Tidal Basin Review,* as well
as many others. She has received support from the Maryland State
Arts Council, the MacDowell Colony, Vermont Studio Center, and
Yaddo, and teaches at Goucher College, in Baltimore.

The New Issues Poetry Prize

Kerrin McCadden, *Landscape with Plywood Silhouettes*
2013 Judge: David St. John

Marni Ludgwig, *Pinwheel*
2012 Judge: Jean Valentine

Andrew Allport, *the body | of space | in the shape of the human*
2011 Judge: David Wojahn

Jeff Hoffman, *Journal of American Foreign Policy*
2010 Judge: Linda Gregerson

Judy Halebsky, *Sky=Empty*
2009 Judge: Marvin Bell

Justin Marks, *A Million in Prizes*
2008 Judge: Carl Phillips

Sandra Beasley, *Theories of Falling*
2007 Judge: Marie Howe

Jason Bredle, *Standing in Line for the Beast*
2006 Judge: Barbara Hamby

Katie Peterson, *This One Tree*
2005 Judge: William Olsen

Kevin Boyle, *A Home for Wayward Girls*
2004 Judge: Rodney Jones

Matthew Thorburn, *Subject to Change*
2003 Judge: Brenda Hillman

Paul Guest, *The Resurrection of the Body and the Ruin of the World*
2002 Judge: Campbell McGrath

Sarah Mangold, *Household Mechanics*
2001 Judge: C.D. Wright

Elizabeth Powell, *The Republic of Self*
2000 Judge: C.K. Williams

Joy Manesiotis, *They Sing to Her Bones*
1999 Judge: Marianne Boruch

Malena Mörling, *Ocean Avenue*
1998 Judge: Philip Levine

Marsha de la O, *Black Hope*
1997 Judge: Chase Twichell